21 ELEMENTS OF JUSTICE

TOM CLIFFORD

Order this book online at www.trafford.com
or email orders@trafford.com

Most Trafford titles are also available at major online book retailers.

Print information available on the last page.

ISBN: 978-1-6987-1103-4 (sc)
ISBN: 978-1-6987-1104-1 (e)

Trafford rev. 02/11/2022

www.trafford.com
North America & international
toll-free: 844-688-6899 (USA & Canada)
fax: 812 355 4082

Criminal Justice-The Twenty-one Factors

Tom Clifford

The author, a non-attorney, would like to see more, in the popular literature, on the reasons why this society administers "justice" the way it does. To the victims, "justice" is a blurred emotional concept: "find him, bring him to justice!, punish him!"..... "Mother said her child was beaten by the school counselor, and she demands justice!" "nail that murdering bastard and burn him!" . In contrast, the law must be rational and transparent. Why are certain acts defined as specific crimes, why are they variably enforced, and why are specific "punishment" decisions made and actions imposed? I would like to explore the rationales in an understandable format, to help the public know why we do what we do. This essay is not to be considered profound or detailed... it is just a plea for help.

The author sees **twenty-one** separate, distinguishable factors in the application of "justice". They are described below, in no particular order. These factors should be thoughtfully and publicly examined. "Justice" encompasses legislation, apprehension, investigations and arrest, charges that are filed, prosecution, jury selection and instructions, bail, sentencing, incarceration, probation / parole decisions, case management, and more. Proper administration of justice would require that each of these actions be driven by one or more of those twenty-one factors, specific to each case. The reasoning should be articulated and transparent. Certainly now and in centuries past, all these factors have been combined, and balanced, in an attempt to "make the punishment fit the crime", but typically the rationale is neither expressed nor documented, nor consistent, at least within the public's awareness. A thoughtful discussion of these reasonings might lead to a better public understanding and support of our brand of justice, to actions and possibly legislation to optimize and make consistent sentencing and case-management guidelines, and perhaps lead to better public understanding and support of law-enforcement decisions. This essay is intended to trigger such a discussion.

The section below identifies each of the twenty-one factors. Later sections expand on these, and offers examples and questions arising from recent news and TV reports. A later section offers a summary and recommendations.

These twenty-one factors are, in no particular order:

1. Deterrence. Convince him and others not to do that again, or he'll get in worse trouble.

2. Isolation / containment. Take him off the streets so he cannot do that again. Keep the public safe.

3. Punishment ... make him hurt! Make him remember this! make him hate it!

4. Personal vengeance. You hurt me (or a loved one), so I want to hurt you!

5. Societal vengeance and outrage . We all hate what you've done. We all feel hurt/disgusted/vulnerable/etc.

6. Restitution You must pay me/us back for what you stole or damaged!

7. Rehabilitation. We'll get you healthy/educated/socialized/ etc,. so later you will benefit yourself and society.

8. Proportionality. The punishment must fit the crime.

9. Politics, local and national. "....he's soft on crime! I'm not! ...." "...they need help, not punishment ...."

10. Government / social policy. Certain actions, such as treason, espionage, national security exposure, environmental damage, etc. will not be tolerated.

11. Knowledge of the victim The race, wealth, fame, position of the aggrieved/victim could be a factor.

12. Knowledge of the accused (mentally competent? provoked? under the influence?) extremely biased; all could be a factor.

13. Severity/extent/scope of the crime; within the letter of the law. Is a "hate" crime more severe than just your average bad act?

14. Externalities in the system: understaffing, prison overcrowding, facilities, etc. could be a factor.

15. "Restorative Justice". A theory and practice connecting perpetrator and victim, to facilitate change, understanding, healing, and acceptance.

16. Compassion. The victim and/or society feel, after time passes, that the criminal deserves a more lenient treatment. Is "morality" part of this?

17. Changes in the law Society and its laws often evolve to an altered view of "justice" in certain cases.

18. Changes in the criminal/accused. Good behavior, remorse, outreach, conversion, etc. could be a factor.

19. Bias (personal, regional, religion, racial, cultural) within the applications of justice, by the police, DA, judge, jury, Parole office, etc.) Pardons for certain offenses can reflect bias of governing entities.

20. Strength of the Evidence At the moment of arrest, or in decisions to prosecute, or credibility of witnesses in court or decisions by a jury; all hinge on the perceived clarity and quality of the evidence.

21. Competence or capacity of Administrators. An attorney's "incompetence", or a defense team is deep and well-funded compared to the prosecutor's team, or a judge facing "judicial misconduct", etc. could all be cause for appeal or reversal.

Expanding these a bit:

1. Deterrence. Convince him and others not to do that again, or he'll get in bad trouble..... prevent other similar crimes. Trespassing and sexual harassment in the workplace can likely be deterred, if the potential violators know that they'll get in trouble if they do it. The restaurateur will incorporate wheel-chair access features and will properly clean up his kitchen, if he knows for sure he will lose his license if he doesn't. Oil tankers will operate and equip properly if the owners know they will face fines far greater than their profits, if they cause oil pollution. The objective here is an attempt to deter similarly situated persons or entities from committing the same or similar crimes. The punishment must be sure and well-publicized: the act will be detected, and punishment will be enforced; the act will have grievous consequences. The consequence must be far harsher than any criminal gain associated with the act. Clearly this objective is case-specific: the CEO will be deterred from violation of insider-trading laws if he knows he will surely face prison time. However, the repeat child-molester will not be deterred in his heinous quest by the prospect of possible arrest and incarceration. Deterrence would not a factor in sentencing in that case.

2. Containment /isolation. ...keep 'em off the streets, safely locked away. This would appropriately apply to child abusers, multiple DUI offenders, serial killers, etc. The objective here is primarily to isolate the person from society..... to

keep society safe ... to provide society the knowledge and confidence that this criminal is no longer a threat, at least during the time he is incarcerated. Certainly others of the several reasons could apply that might impact the conditions of isolation, but the detention reason is to protect society from this particular person. The crime determines whether this objective applies: The check-kiter and stock manipulator are no threat to kids on the block ... detention would not be a factor in that instance .... whereas the obsessed serial killer sociopath and child-molester are clear threats, and society must be protected ... the criminal must be isolated/contained.

3. Punishment ... make him hurt! Make him remember this! make him hate it! make him regret what they did. The criminal must be made to feel pain, physical/emotional/psychological, or all three. "He got what he deserved!" This punishment must be swift and sure, and clearly related to the offence. Society at this moment must punish the bad guy for what he did. Deterrence might happen as a bonus, but the primary motive is to ensure that the criminal feels the pain. Note that simple incarceration may not constitute an adequate hurt. For instance: a young gang-banger might feel a prison term is a necessary and welcome rite-of-passage, solidifying his street-cred stature among his peers, and providing a useful opportunity for net-working and "job-skills" training . The Aryan Brother skin-head also might not mind very much... his psychological needs might be satisfied nicely in the company of kindred spirits. The conditions

within incarceration should be much more onerous than conditions encountered outside. Public whippings and worse, over the centuries, have fulfilled that objective of punishment. Do the crime and you will suffer.

4. <u>Personal vengeance</u>. You hurt me (or a loved one), so I want to hurt you! <u>The sentence got him</u> what he deserved .... we (society and the victim) are satisfied. The criminal has hurt a victim and by extension has hurt all of us. We need to feel that justice has been served, that we have done our part to punish the criminal. We must be satisfied at sentencing; forgiveness or understanding might arise later. Society's need for cathartic vengeance is rarely stated, but is a real element in the human make-up. Certainly this taste for vengeance varies substantially among individuals and cultures, and can change within an individual or a criminal's situation over time; and the willingness to articulate it is also variable, but the reality of it must be acknowledged and considered. Further, the passage of time and behavior during incarceration could shift society's position... the blazing passion for vengeance could subside, and be replaced by a compassionate offer of rehabilitation for a now-well-behaved strong-arm robber. That shift in reasonings also needs to be examined and articulated as a specific case evolves.
You hurt me (or a loved one), so I want to hurt you!

5. Societal vengeance and/or outrage. He got what he deserved .... we (society and the victim) are satisfied. The

criminal has hurt a victim and by extension has hurt all of us. We need to feel that justice has been served, that we have done our part to punish the criminal. We all hate what you've done. We feel hurt / disgusted/ vulnerable / etc. We must be satisfied at sentencing ..... forgiveness or understanding might arise later. Society's need for cathartic vengeance is rarely stated, but is a real element in the human make-up. Certainly this taste for vengeance varies substantially among individuals and cultures, and can change within an individual or a criminal's situation or culture over time; and the willingness to articulate it is also variable, but the reality of it must be acknowledged and considered. Further, the passage of time and behavior during incarceration could shift society's position... the blazing passion for vengeance could subside, and be replaced by a compassionate offer of rehabilitation for a now-well-behaved murderer. That shift in reasonings also needs to be examined and articulated as a specific case evolves. Somebody opined that "prison terms are precisely to pay one's debt to society"

What does that mean?

6. <u>Restitution</u> You must pay me or us back for what you stole or damaged, as restitution .Pay $$$ back to the aggrieved. This one is straightforward. The aggrieved, an individual or the state, deserves recompense for damages. The victim must be made whole, he must be satisfied. Certainly money can figure into other reasonings, for which incarceration is inappropriate. These could include fines used as deterrence

as well as punitive damages imposed as a punishment. That is not relevant in this sense. Certainly the structure of the restitution is case-specific and is often complex; but somehow the victim should be compensated, and by the criminal, not the state. In some cases the state/public itself is the victim (tax evasion for example), and must be compensated. Note importantly also that this factor works both ways: the improper application of "justice" by society's administrators of justice" can be a cause for restitution or reparations to the aggrieved.

7. Rehabilitation (at societies expense!). We'll get you healthy / educated / trained / re-socialized / etc., so you won't mess up again, and so you will benefit yourself and society ....make them useful citizens. Certain criminals may deserve society's help to become contributing citizens. This can include counseling, medical treatment, dependency remediation, basic education, job-skills or parenting training, etc. This effort can be humanitarian: a single mom deserves help off drugs and back into school, to benefit herself and the baby. Or the effort can be coldly practical: the cost of reclaiming and rehabilitating a young gang-banger wanna-be could be far less than the later costs to society of his life of crime and incarceration. Other individuals appear to be beyond help. Efforts for them would not benefit society. A cost-benefit analysis to arrive at this differentiation is difficult but crucial. The decision to provide re-hab support must be made at sentencing; and this decision must be periodically

reviewed during incarceration, and possibly beyond in post-incarceration management. The concept that "society's sole purpose in criminal administration is to help the criminal" must be thoughtfully and compassionately explored, and ultimately dismissed or subject to cost-benefit analysis.

8. Proportionality. "The punishment must fit the crime" is a facile phrase to justify the level of some sort of legal action. What is the "fit"? Is "punishment" the operative element? Bad crime deserves harsh justice? Does this apply only to crimes that "deserve punishment"? Must "rehab support" fit the crime? If this means anything, it should mean "the application of all the aspects of justice must fit the crime, the criminal, the victim, and society" .... all of which is the thrust of this essay. This phrase is too easy and too meaningless to warrant its purported application.

9. Politics, local and national. Politicians get elected or rejected based on their proclamations of "hard on crime" or "we must help these people, not throw them in jail".. The mood of the moment, driven by the party or politics, is often the determinant of law-enforcement actions, from apprehension, thru prosecution and sentencing, into case-management. And that mood changes, and it varies by locale and time. "Sentencing Guidelines" offer generalities, but the extreme differences in the actual application of justice be baffling.

10. Government / social policy. Certain actions such as treason, espionage, national security exposure, environmental, etc

will not be tolerated ... let the world know that we consider this a crime. Certain crimes and sentences are intended to further and enforce and to proclaim government policy. A harsh sentence may apply to an act which, absent international impact, might go un-remarked. Situations involving off-shore financial dealings, terrorism, treason, tax evasion, sex trafficking, trade practices, cyber-hacking, immigration, espionage, environmental issues patent/copyright infringement, pollution, etc,; handled largely under Federal rather than state statutes, typically require these visible policy expressions. Recent example of government policy expression: a foreign government imprisoned two hikers. That government's actions (incarceration, then release) were intended to dramatize its stance on sovereignty, followed by compassion. Our citizens and society are under global scrutiny in international matters. Justice, defined by enforcement and sentencing, applying to our citizens and citizens of other states, must be made visible, and must be shown to be consistent with stated internal and external governmental policy. The world must see how we define and dispense justice, and how we view and possibly influence global justice.

11. <u>Knowledge of the victim</u> The race, wealth, fame, position of aggrieved /victim is (but shouldn't be?) a factor. Assault of an elderly nun or of a rich famous pretty young lady will probably be prosecuted more harshly than prosecution of an identical assault on a homeless beggar. "Our kind of people

don't deserve that". "Make them stop harassing the movie stars". racist? elitist? certainly biased.

12. Knowledge of the accused (mentally competent? provoked? race? under the influence?) is an important factor in the extended application of justice. Was he a basically good guy who just had had a bad day ... or was he a known low-life who should be sent away to keep us all safe? Does he need help for his problems or does he need to be punished? Was the provocation documented and so intense that any one of us would have exploded and committed that act?

13. Severity of the crime, even within the written definition of the crime, severity is a factor. Embezzlement of $1M from a foundation that exists to support homeless and/or disabled folks is seen as much worse that embezzlement of $1M from a billionaire's private account. Murder that includes extended torture and rape will be dealt with particularly harshly. Stealing a pack of cigarettes perhaps should merit a lighter sentence than the theft of something of greater value. There are guidelines for sentencing but these are largely unknown to the public.

14. Externalities within the justice system: understaffing, prison overcrowding, funding of police departments, restrictions due to pandemics, appropriate facilities, etc. Early release of a range of criminalities could mitigate overcrowding. Intense public exposure/coverage of the crime could influence the jury pool. A rich plaintiff could engage expensive attorneys

and many expert witnesses creating burdensome litigation strategies, putting a pro-bono public defender at a severe disadvantage.

15. <u>"Restorative Justice"</u>. This is a theory and practice connecting perpetrator and victim, to facilitate change, understanding, healing, and acceptance. Actions can include mediation between perpetrator and victim, peace-making efforts with contribution from the wider community, community service, assistance for the victim (how can the perpetrator repair the harm...?). These feelings, approaches and actions influence many applications of justice, but they vary widely, and are rarely articulated.

16. <u>Compassion</u>. The victim and society feel, after time passes, that the criminal "deserves" a lesser punishment. "He said he is sorry and I believe him" "Will keeping him in prison bring my son back?" "He did the crime in a moment of confusion and passion, now his children will have no father, and his wife no support for decades; must we punish them too?" Must "justice" be cruel?

17. <u>Changes in the law</u> Society and its laws have evolved and must evolve to altered views of the crime. Racial bias dwindles. The Irish are allowed into certain neighborhoods. Chinese railroad laborers are not jailed for trying to escape. Japanese are not rounded up, Cyber crime is recognized as a growing threat; and legislation, detection, and enforcement

must adapt. Environmental issues and violations require new applications of justice.

18. <u>Changes in the criminal</u>. Good behavior, remorse, outreach, conversion, etc. He is a better person now. He has matured and done everything in prison to improve his life and his value to society. Must he remain in prison because he murdered three innocent persons when he was young and before his teen-age brain had fully developed? Many of those thoughts could be considered. In his case management.

19. Bias (personal, regional, cultural) within enforcement (police, DA, judge, jury, parole office, etc). For an example: A particular community down South has had for a hundred years a problem with black folks, and this unexpressed feeling permeates all their applications of "justice" there. Justice seems to operate differently comparing a rich white-collar murder vs the murder of a nameless black person. Hispanics struggling across our borders to escape intolerable conditions at home are viewed as alien invaders and treated as such. Certain policemen, after years of duty, seem to apply a stereotype view of street encounters. Is that bias or just good judgement based on experience? Finding an un-biased jury of local citizens can be problematic and a request for a change of venue is often encountered.

20. The Strength of Evidence is pivotal, all thru the process. Did a credible witness see that particular person do the act, or was somebody just glimpsed in the area at the time? Was

testimony provided by an expert on DNA evidence? Were fingerprints matched appropriately? Was a police report filed? Was there a guilty plea?

21. <u>Competence</u> Judges and juries can be mistaken or be overwhelmed by new-technology. A recent case involved the new technology available to edit/revise what was purported to be an evidence photograph or video of the scene. This confused or influenced the judge and likely influenced the jury. How can this new-technology problem be rectified?

The sections below are examples and questions arising from recent news and TV reports. Names and details have been changed or omitted. Each one, I hope, exemplifies a law-enforcement action that could benefit from transparency and explanation. I'm faintly aware of rules and guidelines, such as Federal Sentencing Guidelines, but nothing I've found specifically controls or even covers the areas of my concern.

A rich person was sentenced to only five months behind bars for paying half a million dollars in bribes to fraudulently get his two daughters into college. The judge said that prison sentence "is sufficient but not greater than necessary punishment under the circumstances. You were not stealing bread to feed your family". Is punishment the only factor here? I'm suggesting deterrence should be another factor.

A state Supreme Court upheld a life sentence for a man caught stealing hedge clippers from a hardware store. Reason: that state had set life sentences for fourth felony convictions. Why? Is that sentence an effective deterrent? Is society seeking vengeance? This is certainly keeping him off the streets. Is this fairly paying back the hardware store owner (restitution)? Does this punishment fit the crime? Not so much. Plus, being practical, the cost of providing room and board for him for decades, could have been considered. Another plus: perhaps a procedural technicality prevented a proper sentence being imposed. If so, that's another element to be considered in the application of justice.

Somebody said "…prison terms are to "pay one's debt to society." Inmates should be allowed a fresh start, without all those no-vote, no-job, no-housing restrictions following them for life. This country is for redemption and forgiveness,". That's only one person's opinion, and ignores or minimizes all the other elements of justice.

Newspaper report: Ex-convicted gang-banger now employed as re-hab counselor. Traditionally, prosecutors focus on punishment of violent offenders, but this man seeks to give offenders (typically addicts) what they need (drug treatment, education, housing) to live productively. Are the victims of his violence satisfied? Is deterrence satisfied?

"He got 5 months; but could have been sentenced to up to 20 years. Other parents in similar situations also pled guilty and showed remorse, and got similar short sentences. Sentences of white-collar perps and crimes can be influenced by a "show of remorse". Is this justice?

Two folks were arrested and sentenced for chopping down a big rare heritage tree in a state park, outside their property line, to sell it for firewood.. They said there was no ill intent …. they just wanted to make some money. .Societal outrage and government policy at play here

---

"Heinous. Horrendous. Horrible. Unspeakable. Hard to comprehend." Judge used these words to describe the murder of an infant at the hands of the killer before sentencing him to life in prison. "What you did on this day when you killed this baby was an act that is as bad as a human can commit," he said. Several elements of justice at play here, including the nature of the crime.

A public comment: "… solitary confinement has no re-habilitation value …." This comment suggests that the sole justification for solitary is for re-hab. Odd!

A judge said she was honored to sentence him to die in prison, and to be himself repeatedly sexually assaulted, for his sexual abuse crimes. justice or vengeance?

Murderer of 24 people can be considered for parole now after 39 years in prison. "Compassion" vs vengeance, societal outrage, and other elements'

.".....He killed four people! He terrorized the city! The people want justice!" societal vengeance.

Comments on a murderer's case: "...prison won't do him any good," "...he needs to be in a mental hospital with therapy, counseling, meds ..." "... he cannot control his impulses...". "... if he can be helped, don't send him to prison..." This is knowledge of the convict plus compassion, ignoring other elements.

Second DUI, killed three people in traffic offense, sentenced to 47 years. Victim's family says " ...justice was done..." Prosecutor says ".....because of the harm he did to that family, life in prison is fair.....". A statement of proportionality?

Juries sometimes decide outside the law. They ask "Is the consequence/punishment consistent with the act...?" proportionality?

Convicted multiple killer had collected much money thru several programs, but had given almost none of that to any of his victim's family as the court-ordered restitution. This restitution is being rectified thru further legal actions .

A fund-raiser suggests that too many people go to prison for too long for no good public safety reason. Is the prime reason for imprisonment to protect the public? Simplistic and missing several points.

A father raged against a DA, who as an application of some sort of compassion action, recommended sentencing the killer to only a few years in prison. "The father said the DA's action does not protect the citizens and ensure justice!....! " He further asserted that:" .....the city has a DA and public defenders aiding criminals; while crime victims and residents have no one fighting for them.... "the application of" justice must be balanced and transparent.

The victim's bother in court, told the murderer that God would forgive him, and that he wants the best for you, because that's what his bother, the victim, would have wanted . This extreme example of compassion might influence later legal actions.

A mother was seen shoving her 5-yr-old daughter out of the car, near a local zoo, and driving away. She was arrested and charged with felony child abandonment. Society outrage operates here .... deterrence, restitution, isolation, and other elements of justice appear to be irrelevant as this case moves forward.

A woman threatened people at a gay night club, pulling a knife, shouting gay slurs, sentenced to prison. Was this a "hate" crime?

A sanctuary-icon prisoner with many felony convictions was released, then he murdered an innocent tourist. Was his release related to a change in the law, or to sanctuary-city politics? Headlines for this reportage: "Was Justice Served?" We must understand that Judges and PO officers cannot see the future, but laws must accommodate all the elements of justice, including a view of likelihoods.

Headline: "Son Slain at School; Father Seeks Justice … ". Five suspects were seen, one pulled a gun and gunned him down after angry words were exchanged. Parent says "I want them all to get the death penalty" That's personal vengeance!

A school teacher was charged with 16 counts of sexually assaulting two children under 10 yrs old.. He's awaiting trial, Social and personal vengeance, as well as isolation is relevant here.

Editorial. "40% of condemned killers have spent at least 19 years on death row...." "... this rarity of executions removes its value as a deterrent. "...this death sentence has no practical effect .... "" ...better to put resources into prosecuting cases; 40% of homicides remain unsolved ; killers on the street are more dangerous that killers on death row..." This editorial mixes many concepts: practicality, deterrence, social/personal vengeance, punishment, etc.

Youthful murderer in this state was sentenced as an adult. Attorney says the offender "won't get the help she needs ..... Juvenile court would have provided the appropriate social and mental health services..." This suggests that the overriding application of "justice" is to help people. Does murder entitle one to state-funded mental health treatment?

Gangster stabs five people, gets seven year sentence reduced to 1½ years because of "good time" (even though while in jail he assaulted another prisoner!) . Jails are overcrowded because of insane drug laws; and this gangster will soon be again out on the streets.!!!!! Deterrence? Punishment? Protect society? What were the elements leading to this decision?

An impassioned quote: "how long does someone have to be in prison, before he is rehabilitated?" that's NOT the reason he is in prison!

A crab fisherman was fined $47,000 for bringing in some undersized Dungeness Crabs (2.3% of the haul vs max 1% by law), That was overturned and reduced by a judge who said that fine was "grossly disproportionate". Maybe proportionality was at play here.

2-yr old kid was killed by pit bull. The owner, a close relative, faces 10-yr sentence for child endangerment. Grieving family expresses compassion. Prosecutors say this sort of case arises frequently, and that juries face a guilty or not-guilty understandable decision dilemma, What "justice' elements will be operative here?

Lady convicted of DUI hit and run murder gets 55-to-life sentence. She had a continuing life history of drug and alcohol intoxication, Victim's family expressed/wanted and got vengeance, Did victim's "vengeance". affect that sentence?

An incarcerated murder convict started helping authorities, took counseling and classes, expressed remorse, etc., and got his sentence reduced to time served. Is this "justice"? Did that satisfy personal and societal vengeance? Does this satisfy deterrence and other elements? Who decided?

Lethal injection for executions is under review process, to reduce/eliminate the convict's pain. Some say, however, that the victim's pain should not be forgotten. Should personal and social vengeance as well as proportionality be considered?

Convicted of attempted murder of four police officers, saying at trial that he had wanted to kill as many people as possible, He got sentenced to 400 years ....is that fair and proportional? DA says "...he never showed any remorse ... no reason for a shorter sentence ... it's a fair resolution...". This is a faint attempt at transparency.

Many guns confiscated at the airport. Sentences vary, depending on intent (deliberate or accidental), attitude, previous record, etc. Repeat offenders are very rare. Most offences are accidental. Methods are being considered to provide for more awareness, and therefore better deterrence. Knowledge of the criminal is a factor here.

———————◆◇◆◆◇◆———————

The killer of several churchgoers was given the death sentence, despite several victims family members who advocated leniency, expressing forgiveness and reconciliation. Arguments against the death sentence included doubts of this sentence's morality or its efficacy in deterrence. Society must balance all the elements of "justice"; and there should be some learned discussion .

———————◆◇◆◆◇◆———————

Parole has been denied four times in the case of a Manson follower. The governor said that Manson cult killer still poses an unreasonable danger to society and appears to show no remorse. This is an example of the elements of isolation, apparent knowledge of the criminal, and societal outrage as factors in parole hearings.

———————◆◇◆◆◇◆———————

A big city experiences a rash of home-invasion burglaries. Two multiple-repeat burglary offenders were arrested again and jailed, A local politician muses about incarceration *to prevent them from committing more crimes", or a program of rehab and counseling to help these career criminals overcome their problems. The whole mix of elements of justice are in play here (punishment, isolation, rehabilitation, deterrence, etc.) and there will probably be little transparency as the cases move forward.

Hi-speed collision DUI fatality .... the driver died, engulfed in flames, so the cause of death will be clear. Additionally, the <u>gruesomeness of death will hang over everything</u>. Note that there is never a good way to die, but burned inside a car is certainly a particularly bad way. This is an example of the element of severity/extent/scope becoming a factor in the application of justice. Will that be discussed?

Federal authorities charged a nurse at a local hospital with stealing authentic coronavirus vaccination cards, along with vaccine lot numbers required to make the cards appear legitimate .Action on this crime could pivot on government/social policy, or societal outrage, as well as deterrence.

A "religious" man who was often seen reading the Bible, was arrested and charged with the killings of three people. He had invited them into his motel room and then killed them and dismembered their bodies. He told police that the killings were "sacrifices", and confessed to two other murders. He was sentenced to five life sentences. Factors? Public outrage and the severity of the crime.

State Court upheld a life sentence for a man caught stealing hedge clippers from a hardware store. Reason: the state sets life sentences for fourth felony convictions. Why? Is that an effective deterrent? Is society seeking vengeance? This is keeping him off the streets. Is this paying back the hardware store owner? Does this sentence feel like the punishment fits the crime? Not so much. Plus .... being practical, ... the cost of providing room / board for decades could have been considered. Another plus: perhaps a procedural technicality prevented a proper sentence being imposed. If so, that's another element to be considered in the application of justice.

He was found guilty of racketeering and violating the Mann Act, an anti-sex trafficking law, and accused of sexual exploitation of a child, bribery, kidnapping, among other disturbing crimes. "A predator who used his inner circle to ensnare underage girls and young men for decades in a sordid web of sex abuse, exploitation and humiliation. To the victims: your voices were heard, and justice was served. We hope that today's verdict brings comfort and closure to the victims." Vengeance and punishment and outrage were factors in this application of "justice".

A Navy nuclear engineer with a top secret security clearance and his wife were arrested. They had sent restricted data to an unidentified country, and later began selling secrets for thousands of dollars to an undercover FBI agent posing as a foreign official,. At one point, he had hid a memory card containing documents about submarine nuclear reactors in half a PB&J sandwich, at a "dead drop" location while his wife acted as lookout. Justice factors in handling this case will include societal outrage, government policy ad deterrence, to any future treasonous actors.

Cheating is a third-degree felony. "So for skipping $1.25 toll, he now has a felony charge and record," the DA explains, "we want to let people know it's not worth it, pay the toll or don't use the road." Extreme deterrence gone wild?

An ex-priest was convicted of rape/murder of a parishioner; and was sentenced to life in prison, That seems to satisfy several elements of "justice"

A businesswoman whose Ponzi scheme bilked hundreds of people out of nearly $400 million was sentenced Wednesday to 15 years in federal prison. She received more than the sentence recommended by prosecutors. The judge noted that the victims were friends and neighbors. "This is a serious level of deceit and betrayal". Several elements of justice at play here.

<hr />

A solution to jail over-crowding could be to release eligible pre-trial detainees (PTDs)into an Electronic Monitoring Program (EMP); but the Grand Jury found that EMP for pretrial detainees is not part of the county philosophy. Several County interviewees said that EMP for specific cases could be useful tool in reducing jail populations.; and recommended re-consideration for expanded EMP efforts for PTDs. An example of externalities being considered in justice.

<hr />

Jury ponders… did he understand the nature/quality/legal/moral implications of his act during his crime? If found insane, he would face time in a mental facility, then when found sane, he could go free. That sidesteps other elements of justice. Is it OK for crazy folk to kill? Do the victim's families agree? and proportionality be forgotten?

<hr />

Very early thoughts, from 2012, the beginnings of research into this essay:

Catch phrases:

1. "pay your debt to society"

2. "protect the public"

3. "justice must be done"

4. "he got what he deserved"

5. what's the shelf life of vengeance?

6. when does compassion kick in? if ever? by whom?

7. how / when do advances in medical and psychological knowledge begin, to influence and inform application of "justice"?

8. distinguish between victim's hurt and society's hurt. Different crimes, different time scales, different externalities.

9. what's "cruel and unusual punishment"? give that some thought!

10. solitary for a gang-banger, a state-funded retreat for a rich embezzler. are those fair? proportional?

11. convict's rights. victim's rights. describe/equate/distinguish the two?

12. does every parole board (city/county/state/federal) apply the same decision criteria… all the time?

13. influence of time-and local factors: provocation, situation, culture, politics, history, recent events. etc

14. does the exact mix of "justice" factors continue to operate from all the way from arrest thru adjudication, incarceration, parole, and beyond?

15. what personal characteristics of the perp and what of the victim must be considered, and by whom?

16. how is society defined as a victim? how valid is that?

17. does the jury panel selection and the jury's decision incorporate all the criteria in all the other application points of "justice"

18. is the definition of "justifiable homicide" spelled out anywhere? and do all judges and juries know that? everywhere? all the time? Is this "justice"? Did that satisfy personal and societal vengeance? Is this deterrence for him and similar potential criminals?

Student who used a hidden camera to spy on a gay classmate, (who later committed suicide) was sentenced to only 30 days in jail. Victim's family said "this was way too lenient Judge said "that ought be enough to deter others". Isn't that a narrow view of the situation? The torture of traumatized solitary-confinement prisoners (10 or more years) doesn't end when they are released from solitary into the general prison population. They have been excluded from job-training, and other re-hab / re-intro / mental health programs . They suffer serious PTSD symptoms, paranoia, incapacity to form friendships and trust; and worse; are convinced that "solitary was intended to crush my soul" . Is this the "cruel and unusual punishment," forbade by our Constitution? Do these folks continue to pose a threat to other prisoners? Could they have been released from solitary earlier? There is some suggestion that solitary confinement exists to separate violent folks from committing more violence within the prison. Is solitary the answer to anything else? Are they being punished? Probably societal outrage has long evaporated if it were ever a factor. Transparency?

The CEO as well as several employees committed fraud, involving phony bank and credit card accounts (they called it "sand-bagging), causing clients substantial losses. They were convicted; fines were imposed. But those fines amounted to only a tiny fraction of the firm's revenue or the salaries of the CEO and the other criminals. Thousands of crooked white-collar criminals have little to fear … these modest fines mean little as a deterrent. Prison time would be a deterrent; and law enforcement must bring them to justice.

A murderer was found to have been legally sane when he killed his girlfriend … that's after lengthy expert analyses and testimony, witness' testimony, and jury deliberations. His 25 year sentence was upheld; the victim's family approved. Societal and personal vengeance, and proportionality are all at play here.

Recent headlines about a hate crime. "Family seeks Justice".. Black musician murdered … family wants "justice' …. which means convict him, imprison him. punish him. whatever. We want "justice". This is personal vengeance This feeling might affect decisions by the judge, jury, or later decisions by authorities.

An editorial expressed the opinion about <u>perilous streets:</u> "… something must be done to keep mentally ill, possibly addicted folks off the streets. They are a public danger. Incarceration alone is not the answer…". Clearly, for these homeless addicted folks, punishment and deterrence are irrelevant. An informed public must weigh cost vs benefit of containment, re-hab, de-tox, counseling, special housing, etc. We need facts and specifics to guide decisions on alternatives to prison. "Justice" must weigh all factors and must be clearly discussed.

A murderer of seven people was sentenced to death. Later he expressed "remorse", and also was said to have "diminished mental capacity". These appeared to be factors in his sentence reduction from death to life-in-prison. How, and why, and by whom was this decided? Is drooling and mumbling "I'm sorry" a ticket out of Death Row? Where are the guidelines and the rationale?

A black musician was murdered … three whites were convicted, but not of the hate-crime enhancement. The opinion was expressed that "….I want justice," Apparently the personal vengeance factor did not prevail in the application of justice., possibly because of unexamined specific circumstances. Should the reasoning have been made public? Knowledge of the convicts as well as knowledge of the victim should have been explained.

A baseball player was called the "N"-word and was taunted by white fans... Earlier, fans threw beer cans and bananas at a black player .These fans were only ejected, but were not prosecuted. These were assaults, and warranted criminal prosecution. Are justice guidelines different in a sports stadium? Bias and external factors are apparently at play here, and were not expressed.

There was a discussion of "revenge porn pictures": A relative light sentence was imposed. A local legislator stated "a harsher sentence might be a bigger deterrent" and "….these people are afraid of having something on their public record…" How much leeway does a local judge have in sentencing? What rules does he follow? Are they written somewhere? Does the public have a say? Do sentencing decisions act as deterrence to the actions of these young knuckleheads, who probably do not get any rational outside news?

The aggrieved family recommended community service, not more prison time. They said "he has learned his lesson", he's been punished enough already." That family is surprisingly compassionate. What lesson did he learn: "don't get caught?" "rob/beat/rape only people with forgiving families? Do parents decide sentencing and parole decisions? Where are the guidelines?

"… violent mentally ill offenders need treatment and training rather than jail time…". "People with untreated psychoses can often be reclaimed … most will accept treatment … jail time is expensive and typically counter-productive. Conversely: society need protection from them (isolation) until they might possibly be "reclaimed". Police need training to defuse these situations to avoid the necessity to use lethal force…." Need a balanced statement of these reasonings.

Public outcry re a multiple murder "… He must be convicted!…. he killed four people! he terrorized the city!… the people want justice!" "Justice" in this case is swayed by, and probably will be swayed by public vengeance and outrage, and the severity of the crime".

Local politician, during his trial, was accused of improperly using his staffers to help him publish his book, which had earned him $5M; and he was ordered by the Ethics Commission to relinquish those profits. This seems to be an example of the factors of restitution and possibly deterrence in the furtherance of justice.

A former reality TV star was convicted by a federal jury of <u>downloading and possessing child pornography.</u> He faces up to 20 years in prison and fines of up to $250,000 for each count when he's sentenced. "Regardless of wealth, social status, or fame, our office will continue to seek out all individuals who seek to abuse children and victimize them, through the downloading, possession, and sharing of child pornography," said the U.S. Attorney who prosecuted the case. Societal outrage is a factor here.

Statements that were circulating after a trial of young killers. "deterrence doesn't stop these killers. Containment is necessary. They have no awareness of consequences, The threat of a death sentence isn't an effective deterrent...." They must by kept off the streets, ".... a harsh sentence can bring a measure of closure to the grieving family of the murdered victim..." Personal vengeance and societal outrage could influence "justice" as this case moves forward.

A prosecutor, who opposes the death penalty, stated ".... there's no evidence that executing criminals improves public safety..." The public, grieving and angry, reacted, and that prosecutor was removed from the case. The governor said it's clear that that prosecutor will not fight for justice..." The application of "justice" must accommodate all relevant elements .....

A man released from prison after serving13 years; because the forensic data and crucial evidence was recanted by a forensic expert. Justice still not served! He is apparently not eligible for the \$100/day compensation for exonerated convicts, because "he was <u>not found innocent, only found not guilty</u>". Strange application of justice and semantics!!! Did this decision pivot on incompetence, or on knowledge of the "criminal, or what??

The governor commuted the sentences of six people convicted of murder, and three others for attempted murder or kidnapping. He said they showed remorse and great personal growth while incarcerated; and thus deserved a second chance.. Another murderer asked for and received clemency, saying "I cannot change the past but I've repented; and several more murderers received clemency / reduced sentences because, in the governors opinion, they were model prisoners, and had received educations and had done good works while in prison. Astonishing elevation of "remorse and growth" to subvert the original elements that had informed the earlier sentences! Would this be a cynical tactic for other murderers to shorten their sentences?

A very clear case of judicial bias and/or incompetence. This is the most extreme sentence I've ever seen for a drug case," state policy director for a criminal justice reform group. The judge sentenced a young black drug offender to consecutive prison times, way beyond the prosecutor's recommendation, effectively imposing a life sentence. This deeply red county is known for harsh sentences for Black and brown offenders. Institutional bias, ... is this element of "justice"?

. Outrage! A judge sentenced a man who had raped his 12-yr-old daughter to serve only 2 months in a local jail. The judge said the defendant could be treated, could be rehabilitated, and needs no lengthy imprisonment. "...He needs no lengthy imprisonment...????! So far, 82,000 signatures have been recorded for wanting this judge to be impeached and removed. The man "deserves only re-hab", at society's expense? Really? Societal and personal vengeance and outrage at play here. This outrage might be expressed in later appeals, or in how he might be treated by other inmates in the local jail.

Some well-meaning outsider stated confidently that "... prison terms are precisely only to pay one's debt to society ..." Really? He opined that all ex-felons should upon release have all citizenship privileges restored.. Is the "debt to society" defined so narrowly? Are punishment and deterrence,and all the other elements of justice to be dismissed so readily and without any discussion?

"....she will be at every court hearing, to ensure justice is served, on behalf of XXXXXX...". She advocates severe punishment for the murderer of XXXXX. This is an example of vengeance as a possible element of the application of "justice", as this case goes forward.

"but if his condition had been treatable, should he have been sent to prison? "A fund-raiser pamphlet asks if too many people go to prison for too long for no good public safety reason. This suggests that the prime reason for imprisonment is to protect the public. A public comment:: "... solitary confinement has no re-habilitation value .... The full meaning of justice is that he'd be rehabilitated. I don't know who he is, but I hope he gets the help he needs." Comments on a specific murder's case: "… prison won't do him any good," "…he needs to be in a mental hospital with therapy, counseling, meds …" "… he cannot control his impulses…". "… if he can be helped, don't send him to prison…" Letter to editor: "…prison terms are to pay one's debt to society … former inmates should be allowed a fresh start, without those no-vote, no-job, no-housing restrictions following them for life." This country is for redemption and forgiveness …. "Knowledge of the prisoner and compassion and rehab seem to be at work here, but some might argue that's not enough," These comments suggest that the only justification for incarceration and imprisonment is for re-hab. Odd!

"…..He killed four people! He terrorized the city! The people want justice!….." societal vengeance might influence the follow-up application of justice

A multiple sexual predator, was given a reduced sentence, and was not required to register as a sex offender, because "he had taken an anxiety drug that had side effects of hypersexuality and reduced impulse control". Prosecutors were stunned and victims were outraged. Is "knowledge" of the criminal, or judicial incompetence, at play here?

"A murder conviction gives a sense of justice to the family of the victim"

Federal court states the death penalty system "serves no legitimate purpose". Can he or anyone state what that "legitimate purpose" is?

Letter to editor: reader notes that "two cold-blood killers were sentenced to only 8 yrs in prison ... was the victim's life that cheap? ". Proportionality and societal vengeance are at play here .... what is a life worth?

Toddlers loose on freeway, cars screeching to stop, nobody hurt at all, kids herded back to play-school, cops talking to unaware teacher who said "the latch on the gate was confusing and must have popped open". What is the crime and the justice element here? Is inattention and incompetence a crime in an accident like this? What if one of the kids had been hurt/killed?

A governor pardoned hundreds of convicts, most in prison because of violent crimes (murder, rape, etc.). His clemency outraged many folks, especially the victims. He stated that "the state does not carry out vengeance on their behalf". He believes in "a second chance and forgiveness". Clearly he has his private views on all the operative elements of justice. On a practical note, he observed that reducing jail facilities, supervision, medical coverage, etc., saves lots of money, plus alleviates overcrowding. That is more understandable but still not defensible.

Each jurisdiction has its own money / budget / facility / needs problems. Is "justice" (cost/benefit) applied evenly and over time?

Someone please explain "cruel and unusual punishment" and "humane treatment" in the context of a horrible brutal rape/ murder. Does proportionality (let the punishment fit the crime) fit in here? Is the act itself or the consequence of the act the operative factor in prosecution and beyond? Inadequate snuffing of a campfire or intentional arson ..... vs widespread death and $ costs, caused by a major wildfire? Proportionality?

Student who used a hidden camera to repeatedly spy on a gay classmate, (who later committed suicide) was sentenced to only 30 days in jail. Victim's family and others said that was "way too lenient". Judge said "that ought be enough to deter others". Isn't that a narrow view of the situation?

Comment "...... solitary confinement has no re-hab value!..." That speaker suggests that a sentence should be based solely on society's obligation to rehabilitate a multiply-offending criminal. Why else would he have been sentenced to solitary?). Do we owe them that? How about all the other elements? Several other factors were doubtless involved in the decision to put him in solitary. The prime one was probably to confine him to protect other prisoners and/or guards. Other factors could have been punishment as well as to deter other "what have I got to lose?" convicts from in-prison violence.

An idiot teenager stuffed a cat inside a washing-machine. The cat died. The court banned him from keeping, owning or participating in the care of animals for five years and said the detention order was justified because he had caused "prolonged suffering" that led to the death of the pet; as well as to have caused extreme distress to the cat's owners. Authorities said: "This was a very distressing and sad case for us to deal with . "We will always take a strong stance against animal abuse, cruelty and neglect; and if necessary we will take the perpetrators to court" . Societal outrage at play here.

Very early thoughts, from 2012, the beginnings of my research into this essay:

1. "pay your debt to society"?

2. "protect the public"?

3. "justice must be done"?

4. "he got what he deserved"

5. what's the shelf life of vengeance?

6. when does compassion kick in, if ever?

7. how / when do advances in medical and psychological knowledge begin to influence and inform application of "justice"?

8. distinguish between victim's hurt and society's hurt. Different crimes, different time scales, different externalities.

9. what's "cruel and unusual punishment"? give that some thought!

10. solitary for a gang-banger? a state-funded retreat for a rich embezzler. is that fair? proportional?

11. convict's rights. victim's rights. describe/equate/distinguish the two?

12. does every parole board (city/county/state/federal) apply the same decision criteria... all the time?

13. influence of time-and local factors: provocation, situation, culture, politics, history, recent events. etc

14. does the exact mix of "justice" factors continue to operate all the way from arrest thru adjudication, incarceration, parole, and beyond?

15. what personal characteristics of the perp and what of the victim must be considered, and by whom?

16. how is society defined as a victim? how valid is that?

17. does the jury panel selection and the jury's decision incorporate all the criteria in all the other application points of "justice"

18. is the definition of "justifiable homicide" spelled out anywhere? and do all judges and juries know that? everywhere? all the time?

19. a "Sentencing Commission" studies the "science of sentencing; best practices" '' ....the traditional focus on punishing criminals has failed us all...".. "....how to minimize recidivism and boost public safety...." "...who should be steered out of the system by education, addiction therapy, mental health treatment...'

More early thoughts early in beginning of this project

>When does revenge recede and compassion/tolerance begin?

>Who decides cost/benefit when planning penal decisions and facilities?

>What training do judges and prosecutors and enforcement folks get?

>Describe jury nullification; how do juries often subvert the law?

>Can "jail overcrowding" impact the application of "justice"?

>Can a judge say to the jury "ignore the victim, concentrate on the crime?

>Investigator looks at murderer's rehab in penal/parole systems ... described grief and vengeance of victim vs the murderers' remorse, growth and maturity .... noted that 1000 murderers freed after 20 years in prison: "not one has murdered again" ....convicts who "pose no risk to society" remain incarcerated, at society's expense

>Argument: wheel-chair bound terminally ill 33-year-incarcerated killer deserves a "mercy" release ....vs ....." the convict upon release would still be still capable of murder. Who decides?

This concludes my little essay. I'm hoping somebody in the legal world can expand on these thoughts.........

Tom Clifford 1-30-2021

Printed in the United States
by Baker & Taylor Publisher Services